roses

ANTONIA SWINSON

roses

beautiful ideas for home and celebration

RYLAND
PETERS
& SMALL

LONDON NEW YORK

Senior designer Sally Powell

Senior editor Clare Double

Picture researcher Emily Westlake

Production Deborah Wehner

Art director Gabriella Le Grazie

Publishing director Alison Starling

First published in the United States
in 2004
by Ryland Peters & Small, Inc.
519 Broadway, 5th Floor
New York NY 10012
www.rylandpeters.com

10 9 8 7 6 5 4 3 2 1

ISBN 1 84172 565 X

Printed and bound in China

Library of Congress Cataloging-in-Publication Data

Swinson, Antonia.
  Roses : beautiful ideas for home and celebration /
Antonia Swinson.
     p. cm.
  ISBN 1-84172-565-X
  1. Rose arrangements. 2. Roses. 3. Rose
culture. I. Title.
  SB449.3.R67S85 2004
  635.9'33734--dc22

2003015580

contents

introduction

Roses are the queens of the floral world. These venerable plants have been grown and traded since ancient times. Over the centuries, societies have imbued roses with complex symbolism, incorporating them into art and literature, and using them for worship, pleasure, and healing. The secret of the world's love affair with the rose

must surely be its sheer beauty—the intricate form, glorious color, and extraordinary scent, which take the breath away and lift the spirits. But perhaps the greatest wonder is that most of these stunning plants are as robust as they are ravishing, meaning that anyone can have a little bit of paradise in their own backyard.

rose essentials

The air was fragrant with the sweet olive,
myrtle and gardenia. There were old-
fashioned roses; the cinnamon, the York and
Lancaster, the little white musk, and the sweet
or Damascus. The glowy-leaved Cherokee
clothed the walls with its great white disks.

Harriott Horry Ravenel, *Charleston: The Place and the People*

roses in the garden

Hundreds of roses are available to the modern gardener, from miniatures to giant ramblers, encompassing varieties that are both centuries old and brand new.

Many of the roses we grow in our gardens have ancient origins. There are Gallica roses, grown by the Greeks and Romans; Damasks, supposedly taken to Europe by the Crusaders from the Middle East; and Albas, probably from southern France and dating back to the Middle Ages. The Musk Rose was probably introduced to Europe from western Asia in the time of Elizabeth I (1533–1603), and Centifolias are the rounded roses often shown in the paintings of the Dutch Masters. In the eighteenth century, Old Roses were crossed with roses brought back from China to create new

varieties such as Chinas and Bourbons. This process of breeding has continued down the centuries, most recently resulting in English Roses, developed by crossing old varieties with modern ones to unite the best features of both.

It is possible that roses grew in the Hanging Gardens of Babylon since there is fossil evidence that they've thrived in Mesopotamia for millions of years. Other ancient civilizations certainly cultivated them for pleasure: excavations at Pompeii, Italy, suggest that roses were grown in private gardens there. By the Middle Ages, roses were being grown alongside medicinal herbs in monastic gardens, and in the Muslim Arabs' paradise gardens, such as the Alhambra in

Many excellent ancient roses are still available, including 'Celsiana,' a Damask pre-dating 1750; 'Maiden's Blush,' a pre-fifteenth century Alba; the Apothecary's Rose, a venerable Gallica; 'Unique Blanche,' a Centifolia dating to 1775; 'York and Lancaster,' a pre-1551 Damask; and the Burgundy Rose, a Gallica dating back to before 1664.

Granada, Spain. Roses have flourished in gardens ever since, but it was the great English landscape gardener Humphrey Repton (1752–1818) who had the idea of planning separate rose gardens, something the Victorians took to their hearts.

Roses can be grown in mixed beds, as hedges, for ground cover, up walls or over sheds, even in pots. Myriad varieties exist, and this breadth of choice can be bewildering to new gardeners. Old Roses, as their name suggests, are the most venerable. They generally flower once a year, in summer, and are usually strongly perfumed. The group includes Gallicas, Damasks, Centifolias, Albas, and Moss roses. Some Old Roses repeat flower, including China roses, Portlands, and Bourbons. There are climbing roses, which usually repeat flower, and ramblers, which grow

larger and flower once. Modern, repeat-flowering roses have a wider color range than Old Roses and include Shrub roses, Hybrid Teas, Floribundas, and English Roses. There are also small-flowered varieties, such as patio roses, miniatures, and Polyanthas. Most are surprisingly robust and easy to grow, and just a little knowledge will give you the pleasure of growing this queen of flowers.

The thirteenth-century Persian poet Sa'di Shirazi wrote a book of poems and prose called *The Rose Garden*, documenting his travels, which is still read and enjoyed today. In it he writes, "I intended to fill the skirts of my robe with roses … as presents for my friends, but the perfume of the flowers intoxicated me so much that I let go the hold of my skirts."

scent and sensibility

A rose's scent is produced by the volatile essential oils in its petals, which evaporate as the flower opens to create a perfumed atmosphere around it.

A trained palate can detect a wealth of flavors in wine. Equally, a finely tuned sense of smell can discern many subtle variations of fragrance in roses, best appreciated early in the morning or after a summer storm. Connoisseurs can detect apple, balsam, clove, honey, lemon, musk, myrrh, nectarine, orange, raspberry, strawberry, tea, and vanilla. To many, the truest rose scent is damask. This hypnotic scent is most prevalent in Old Roses: Damasks themselves, Gallicas, and Centifolias. The most fragrant include 'Belle de Crécy,' 'Charles de Mills,' 'Fantin-Latour,' 'Gloire de Dijon,' 'Ispahan,' 'Madame Isaac Pereire,' 'Reine des Violettes,' *Rosa* x *centifolia*, *Rosa gallica* var. *officinalis*, 'Souvenir du Docteur Jamain,' and 'William Lobb.'

I know a bank where the wild thyme blows,
Where oxlips, and the nodding violet grows;
Quite over-canopied with luscious woodbine,
With sweet musk-roses, and with eglantine.

WILLIAM SHAKESPEARE, *A MIDSUMMER NIGHT'S DREAM*

Roses have inspired artists and craftsmen both ancient and modern, proving to be one of the most enduring motifs in interior design.

the decorative rose

Flowers of all kinds have been painted since early times—the Egyptians depicted lotuses and daisies, while roses appear in frescoes at Pompeii. Centuries later, the jewel-bright pages of medieval breviaries, books of hours, and other illuminated manuscripts were adorned with roses. The image of the Madonna surrounded by rose bushes occurs in various Renaissance works, by painters such as Stefan Lochner and Martin Schongauer. In Sandro Botticelli's *Primavera*, the goddess Flora holds roses, identified as Gallicas, in her skirts, and it is thought that those in *The Birth of Venus* are the Great Double White and 'Maiden's Blush.' The seventeenth-century Dutch Masters, among them Ambrosius Bosschaert, depicted elegant

Even in modern interiors, the classic rose motif can find a place. Achieve a faded rose chintz effect by soaking fabric in a weak solution of tea.

What's in a name? that which we call a rose
By any other name would smell as sweet.

WILLIAM SHAKESPEARE, *ROMEO AND JULIET*

arrangements of flowers such as tulips, irises, columbines, and, of course, roses (often Centifolias). Roses frequently grace the pretty, airy paintings of eighteenth-century French artists François Boucher and Jean-Honoré Fragonard. In the next century, another Frenchman, Ignace Henri Théodore Fantin-Latour, painted a famous series of roses (a wonderful pink variety is named after him), and although Vincent Van Gogh is usually associated with sunflowers, he painted lots of roses, too.

Floral motifs and patterns have always been used for wallpapers and fabrics. In Europe before the sixteenth century, stylized florals appeared on tapestries, embroidery, damasks, and velvets. The proliferation of floral patterns was encouraged by the importation of the first handblocked calicos (indiennes) from India. Increasingly naturalistic floral patterns became popular in the seventeenth century, while the eighteenth century saw the influence of Eastern ceramics in chinoiserie designs and the production of floral chintzes, developed from calicos. The Victorians were fascinated by the language of flowers and by naturalistic, often overblown, floral designs. In the 1980s there was a revival of interest in chintzes and the English country house look, and the appeal of vintage fabrics continues today.

The vogue for vintage style has seen rose designs
of the eighteenth and nineteenth centuries reworked,
often aged to match the faded charm of the originals.

The rose played many symbolic roles in the ancient world. In classical mythology, Aphrodite, the goddess of love, was born from sea foam and blown by the West Wind to the shores of Cyprus. Where foam fell on the land, white roses grew. Red roses sprang from her blood when she was scratched by the thorns of a white rose bush. Her son, Eros, the god of sexual desire, is sometimes depicted wearing a wreath of roses. Roses took on various symbolic meanings in Roman culture, representing life, death, and eternal life. The Romans awarded rose wreaths to mark military successes, and rose petals were scattered at the feet of victors at the Games. They also used roses at funerals and offered rosebuds to the deceased at their festival of Rosalia. The Romans imported roses from Egypt; bunches of them were discovered in the tomb of King Tutankhamun.

Some roses originate in the Middle East, and the medieval Persians grew them and imbued them with mystical meaning. With the waning of the Roman Empire and the rise of Christianity, the rose was incorporated into Christian symbolism, particularly as an emblem of the Virgin Mary. Eleanor of Provence took her symbol, the white rose, with her from France when she married Henry III of England. Her son, Edward I, also used

In Greek mythology, all roses were thornless until Cupid tried to kiss a bloom and was stung by a bee. In his anger, Cupid shot arrows into the rose bed and the plants have had thorns ever since.

it, but her second son Edmund, first Earl of Lancaster, adopted the red rose. These white and red roses became emotive symbols in the English Wars of the Roses, which ended in 1485 with the union of the houses of York (white) and Lancaster (red) and the emergence of the red and white Tudor rose. The rose is still a symbol of sovereignty and power, and rose oil is one of the ingredients in England's Holy Coronation Anointing Oil.

A rose's scent cannot be synthetically produced; it has hundreds of constituents, some unknown. The oil from the flowers is one of the most expensive—not surprising, since it takes 30,000 blooms to produce half an ounce.

beauty and wellbeing

Many ancient civilizations, including the Egyptians, Persians, Chinese, Mesopotamians, Babylonians, and Greeks, used aromatic mixtures of oils, spices, and plant extracts to anoint their skins, often for religious, as well as sensual, purposes. Roses were among the many exotic ingredients traded in the ancient world; centuries before the birth of Christ, perfumers in Athens used them and other flowers such as lily and iris to make fragrant unguents. Clay tablets excavated from the ancient city of Ur (in modern Iraq) mention the delivery of huge quantities of

rosewater for the Sultan of Baghdad, for perfuming his harem. The Roman emperor Nero apparently showered guests at his extravagant parties with rose petals, and the historian Pliny includes 32 remedies prepared from roses in his *Natural History*. Roses were used extensively by the Arabs in the Middle Ages: rosewater was sprinkled in mosques and added to sherbets and sweetmeats, such as Turkish delight; it was even, with the addition of gum arabic, made into prayer beads.

Rose oil is still used in many of the most luxurious and exquisite perfumes, and in cosmetics. Rosewater makes a soothing toner, and rose oil is said to help dry, mature, or sensitive skin (including conditions such as broken capillaries and eczema). Rose oil is also used by aromatherapists for its therapeutic properties. Damask roses, Centifolia or cabbage roses, and Gallicas are among the varieties most commonly grown as a commercial crop, and the oil they yield is valued for its antiseptic, anti-inflammatory properties and its ability to uplift, easing premenstrual tension, depression, and stress. Rose oil is also said to have aphrodisiac qualities, no doubt the reason why Cleopatra reputedly covered the floors of her palace in rose petals to aid her seduction of Mark Antony!

roses at home

Gather therefore the Rose, whilst yet is prime,
For soon comes age, that will her pride deflower:
Gather the Rose of love, whilst yet is time,
Whilst loving thou mayst loved be with equall crime.

Edmund Spenser, _The Faerie Queene_

Having roses in your home is an affordable luxury, and they are available all year round from florists. With a little care, they last for ages, and with a little imagination they can become stunning displays.

cut and color

Roses are not only a beautiful choice for flower arranging, but also a very practical one. They're sold all year round, everywhere from florists to supermarkets, in one of the widest color ranges available in cut flowers, and they combine harmoniously with many other blooms. They're also good value for money and they last extremely well. The only drawback of roses grown commercially for the floristry trade is that they're usually scentless. If perfume is important to you, you could try asking your florist if they can obtain perfumed varieties or, even better, try growing your own plants. See page 19 for some of the best scented varieties to grow in the garden.

Whether you buy your roses or pick them from your garden, look for strong stems with buds or blooms that are just opening. This will insure the maximum life for your arrangement and give you the pleasure of seeing your roses come into full bloom. If you're cutting your own, do so in the morning before the sun gets too hot, and take a bucket of water with you to plunge the stems into in order to minimize water loss. Before arranging any roses, cut at least an inch off the stems, on a slant to help water uptake. If you've bought a bunch with a sachet of flower food, use it—it does prolong the life of the flowers. If you haven't got any, try adding lemonade, sugar, or soluble aspirin to the water instead. Strip the stems of thorns and leaves that will be below the water line. There are several things you can do to encourage your arrangement to last. To start with, keep all your containers completely clean. Don't put your flowers in direct sunlight or in a draft, and keep them away from fruit—it releases a gas called ethylene, which shortens the life of cut flowers. Remove any dead heads or leaves that appear, and change the water in the container at least every other day. Although a cool atmosphere helps to keep flowers looking good, too cold a room will prevent scented roses from releasing their perfume.

On Richmond Hill there lives a lass,
More sweet than May day morn,
Whose charms all other maids surpass,
A rose without a thorn.

LEONARD McNALLY, *THE LASS OF RICHMOND HILL*

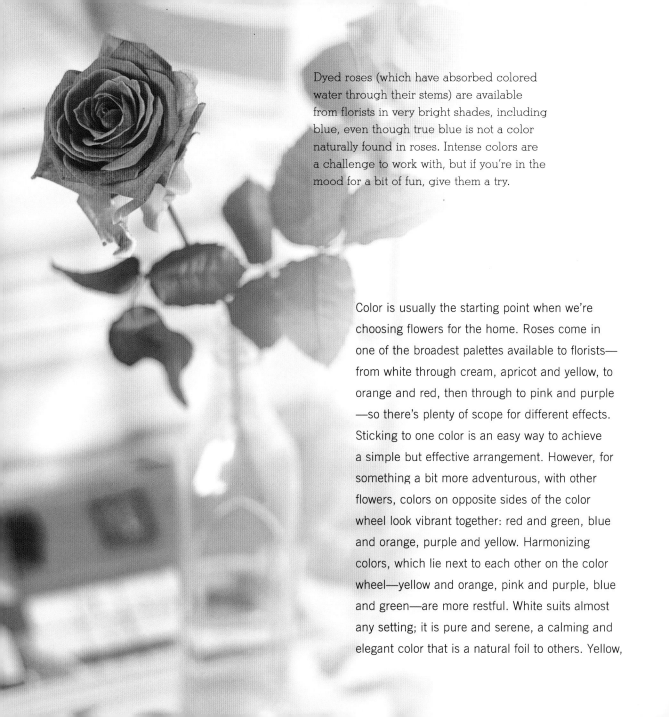

Dyed roses (which have absorbed colored water through their stems) are available from florists in very bright shades, including blue, even though true blue is not a color naturally found in roses. Intense colors are a challenge to work with, but if you're in the mood for a bit of fun, give them a try.

Color is usually the starting point when we're choosing flowers for the home. Roses come in one of the broadest palettes available to florists— from white through cream, apricot and yellow, to orange and red, then through to pink and purple —so there's plenty of scope for different effects. Sticking to one color is an easy way to achieve a simple but effective arrangement. However, for something a bit more adventurous, with other flowers, colors on opposite sides of the color wheel look vibrant together: red and green, blue and orange, purple and yellow. Harmonizing colors, which lie next to each other on the color wheel—yellow and orange, pink and purple, blue and green—are more restful. White suits almost any setting; it is pure and serene, a calming and elegant color that is a natural foil to others. Yellow,

from pale to bright, is like a ray of sunshine, a cheerful, uplifting color and a good partner for white, green, or blue. Orange runs second to red for intensity and warmth. There are roses in bright, zesty oranges, but also the more subtle shades of apricot and peach. Red is perfectly suited to the velvety texture of rose petals. Bright reds look very effective in white, bright rooms; dark, sultry reds and burgundies (which are the closest roses get to black) look at home in an opulent setting or as a dramatic statement against a neutral backdrop. Pink is highly feminine and most of its shades work well together. Pink can also be successfully partnered with purples and lilacs, and even red. Dark purples are dramatic, while lilacs are soft and wistful. In roses, purples tend to be reddish in undertone, so they combine well with crimson and burgundy.

It was not in the winter

Our loving lot was cast!

It was the time of roses,

We plucked them as we passed!

THOMAS HOOD, *IT WAS NOT IN THE WINTER*

A flower arrangement should be a happy
marriage between container and plant. Most
people have a vase or two lurking in a cupboard,
but lots of ordinary things can be turned into
stylish containers, so before you rush out to
buy anything, look around your own home. For
instance, goldfish bowls look stunning filled with
floating flower heads or petals, magnifying their
contents. Wine, ginger ale, mineral water, or
olive oil bottles look particularly good with
one or two stems in them. Try a collection of
bottles in assorted shapes and sizes, lined up

on a mantelpiece or grouped on a table. Look out for pieces of vintage china, which can often be picked up cheaply at secondhand stores, antique markets, and yard sales. An old teapot that has lost its lid becomes an ideal container for a bunch of Old Roses picked from the garden. Milk or cream pitchers are useful, too, and odd teacups are perfect for little posies of spray roses. Spray roses or miniature varieties are also an ideal size for empty perfume bottles, placed on a dressing table or bedside cabinet. Tea glasses, like those used in the Middle East for mint tea, old pieces of colored cut glass, and plain tumblers can be used for small arrangements, perhaps as place markers at a dinner party, or grouped to make a centerpiece. Even humble jelly jars can have charm as flower containers and can be prettied up with narrow ribbon tied around their necks.

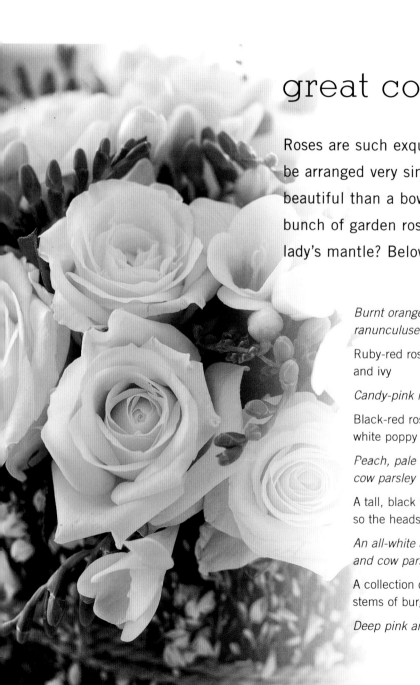

great combinations

Roses are such exquisite flowers that they can be arranged very simply: what could be more beautiful than a bowl full of white blooms or a bunch of garden roses interspersed with frothy lady's mantle? Below are a few more easy ideas.

Burnt orange roses with Iceland poppies and ranunculuses in shades from yellow to vermilion

Ruby-red roses, red amaryllis, winter jasmine, and ivy

Candy-pink roses and lilies

Black-red roses, white ranunculuses, and white poppy anemones

Peach, pale pink, and yellow roses with cow parsley

A tall, black vase filled with white roses cut so the heads sit just above the rim

An all-white arrangement of roses, peonies, and cow parsley

A collection of tall, narrow glass bottles with single stems of burgundy roses and love-lies-bleeding

Deep pink and blue-red roses in a white vase

Try putting a tight cluster of cream roses in a glass jar, then inside a larger glass vase, and filling the space between them with coffee beans.

Pale pink roses, blue bachelor's buttons, and catnip

Pink double lisianthus, pink roses, and pink hydrangea heads

A small, tight bunch of roses, one half pale pink, the other deeper; or one half apricot, the other half tangerine

A red miniature rose plant in a white or silver bowl

A bunch of mixed Old Roses in a vintage teapot

Pink rose heads, packed tightly into a small, decorative bowl

A mixture of pink roses in a group of tea glasses or tumblers

Garden roses, sweet peas, and guelder rose

For Christmas, cream and blue-red roses with any glossy, dark green foliage and berried ivy

Single-color posies in hot pinks and oranges, or pastels, grouped as a centerpiece

Ice-cream pink roses and peonies

Roses in burgundy, ruby red, and deep pink

For winter, cream roses, skimmia leaves, or other evergreen foliage and gold-sprayed twigs

roses for
celebrations

The rose was awake all night for your sake,
Knowing your promise to me;
The lilies and roses were all awake,
They sigh'd for the dawn and thee.

Alfred, Lord Tennyson, *Maud*

Gather ye rosebuds while ye may,

Old Time is still a-flying:

And this same flower that smiles to-day

To-morrow will be dying.

ROBERT HERRICK,

TO THE VIRGINS, TO MAKE MUCH OF TIME

homemade gifts

A handmade present has great charm and is a compliment to the recipient, showing that you've put time and trouble into its creation. Dried rose petals retain their scent and color well and are usually the main ingredient, along with lavender, in the time-honored art of potpourri-making. Other flowers, such as carnations and sweet peas, can be added along with leaves (lemon balm, verbena, scented geranium, marjoram), spices (allspice, cinnamon, nutmeg, vanilla), citrus peel, a fixative (usually orris root), and a few drops of essential oil (which can also be used to revive the

scent if it fades). Potpourri can be presented in a decorative bowl or used to fill sachets. Take a square of fabric or a pretty handkerchief, fill with potpourri, then tie with ribbon and use to freshen shoes, drawers, storage boxes, or closets. Fresh rose petals can be layered with unscented bath salts or talc to make a perfumed treat, which can then be decanted into attractive jars. Rose oil is also useful for scenting gifts, such as soap. Sprinkle the oil onto cotton balls, bind around a bar of unscented soap, and cover with plastic wrap before leaving to mature for six weeks.

Collect roses (open or in bud) on a dry morning when the dew has evaporated. Separate the petals and arrange in a single layer on newspaper, paper towel, or cheesecloth over a cooling rack. Dry away from sunlight and humidity, turning them every day.

Roses are a beautiful addition to any table, whether it's an informal gathering or elegant dinner party. Use varieties that smell as wonderful as they look for a sybaritic experience.

table decorations

Crystallized rose petals are a pretty decoration for cakes and puddings. Use unsprayed petals, pinching off the white "heel" at their base. Lightly beat an egg white and brush onto the petals, then dip in superfine sugar. Dry on a cooling rack in a warm place.

For the unashamedly romantic look shown opposite, peonies, roses, and Singapore orchids have been floated in a goldfish bowl. The glasses also hold rose heads, with petals decorating the plates and table top. A shallow glass bowl filled with rose petals and floating candles would also be atmospheric, casting a soft glow around the table. Alternatively, take a cylindrical vase, fill with crumpled clear cellophane (available from florists), and tuck roses down into it before topping up with water for an effect like cracked ice. Another simple idea is to choose a lovely bowl and fill it completely with blooms to create a domed effect

As late I rambled in the happy fields,

What time the sky-lark shakes the tremulous dew

From his lush clover covert;— when anew

Adventurous knights take up their dinted shields:

I saw the sweetest flower wild nature yields,

A fresh-blown musk-rose; 'twas the first that
  threw

Its sweets upon the summer: graceful it grew

As is the wand that queen Titania wields.

And, as I feasted on its fragrancy,

I thought the garden-rose it far excell'd:

But when, O Wells! thy roses came to me

My sense with their deliciousness was spell'd:

Soft voices had they, that with tender plea

Whisper'd of peace, and truth, and friendliness
  unquell'd.

JOHN KEATS, *TO A FRIEND WHO SENT ME SOME ROSES*

(see far right). If you want to use fewer roses, place a single head on each plate, or pop posies into small vases, tumblers, or glass jars. Small-flowered and spray roses can be arranged in an array of vintage cups and saucers to act as place markers or take-home favors.

An ice bowl looks spectacular and isn't hard to make. Take two plastic or Pyrex bowls, one smaller than the other. Place the small one inside the larger and tape across the tops, making sure the rims are level. Tuck rose petals down the sides (and perhaps sprigs of herbs), then fill carefully with water and freeze. Unmold and fill with summer berries or scoops of ice cream.

Roses can be used in food as well as in decoration; just make sure they are free from chemical sprays, and pinch off the bitter "heel" at the base of the petals before using. Petals can be floated in summer punch, frozen into ice cubes, strewn over salads, or folded into sweetened whipped cream. Using floral waters in cooking dates back to the Middle Ages, and rosewater is still a popular ingredient in Indian and Middle Eastern cuisine. It can be used for custards, icing, jam, jellies, and ice cream, or sprinkled on strawberries for a different taste of summer.

Confectioners in the Middle East closely
guard their recipes for Turkish delight, a
traditional candy of sugar syrup flavored with
rosewater and thickened with cornstarch.

My love is like a red, red rose

That's newly sprung in June;

My love is like the melody

That's sweetly played in tune.

ROBERT BURNS, *MY LOVE IS LIKE A RED, RED ROSE*

Valentine's Day roses

The first commercial Valentine cards were produced in the nineteenth century, but the practice of giving posies of flowers as love tokens began centuries before. Gradually, the choice of flowers came to indicate a special meaning to the recipient. This "language of flowers" reached its height of popularity under the Victorians, who used the code to convey secret messages of passion. Rosebuds meant beauty and youth; red rosebuds, pure and lovely; yellow roses, jealousy or friendship; and the cabbage rose, ambassador of love (see page 61 for more). Red roses were then, as now, an unequivocal symbol of true love, and are still the classic way to say "I love you" on Valentine's Day.

wedding roses

Legend has it that rose oil was first discovered at the
wedding of a Mogul princess. A canal running through
a garden had been filled with rosewater, which separated
in the heat, producing droplets of oil.

Roses and weddings seem to be made for each
other. Both the Greeks and Romans associated
Aphrodite, or Venus, the goddess of love, with
white and red roses. The Romans sprinkled rose
petals on the marriage bed. In the Middle Ages,
roses, grown in secret or enclosed gardens,
became symbolic of the ideals of courtly love.

On a more practical note, roses have many
qualities that make them invaluable to the florist.
Their vast and sumptuous choice of colors,
including ravishing reds and pinks, and delicate

Rose petals, fresh or dried, are a beautiful alternative to rice. Buy flowers or pick your own, then use petals to fill pretty bags, boxes, or paper cones.

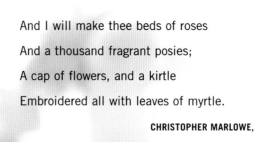

And I will make thee beds of roses

And a thousand fragrant posies;

A cap of flowers, and a kirtle

Embroidered all with leaves of myrtle.

CHRISTOPHER MARLOWE,

THE PASSIONATE SHEPHERD TO HIS LOVE

shades of peach, white and cream, is all tailormade for weddings. Roses are one of the best performers in the cut-flower world, lasting for ages and keeping their good looks intact. They're robust enough to be arranged in all sorts of ways, and can even be sprayed with metallic paint or sprinkled with glitter for exciting effects.

When planning wedding flowers, either bouquets or arrangements, color is usually the starting point. White, with its associations with serenity and purity, is the classic choice, and it can look ethereal or surprisingly dramatic. Yellow is bright and cheerful, while orange is bolder and warmer. Red is intense and fiery, the color of passion. Pink is softer and more feminine; deep purples are regal, and mauves are cooler and more wistful.

With many roses, scent adds another, wonderful sensory dimension, but remember that many of the varieties specially bred for the floristry trade are scentless. If that glorious rose perfume is important to you, make a point of telling your florist, or use garden varieties donated by generous friends.

Roses are versatile flowers, having the ability to look grand and elegant, or charmingly rustic.

They combine beautifully with other flowers or can stand alone, letting their beauty take center stage. A few stems make the simplest and prettiest of posies. They could be hand-tied into a tightly packed dome, with their stems bound in coordinating ribbon or silk. Or they could be mixed with other blooms in a looser style—perhaps red roses with amaryllis, evergreen foliage, and ivy for winter; or sweet peas and ranunculuses for summer. Roses also work very well when made

into a ball, which involves inserting wired blooms in a sphere of florist's foam. Roses' staying power also makes them ideal flowers for boutonnieres.

If roses are the main choice for the bride's flowers, extending their use to the reception will coordinate the look. A single bloom is enough to decorate a folded napkin or a plate at a place setting, or to embellish coffee cups and saucers for the end of the meal. Roses, on their own or with other flowers, last well in table arrangements or could be tucked in among fruit piled on a platter for a striking centerpiece. Floating candles and rose petals could be placed in bowls of water for a highly romantic look, and petals or rose heads can be scattered across table tops. Fresh roses and rosebuds (unsprayed) can also be used to decorate the cake for a final touch.

In the language of flowers, white roses mean eternal love or innocence; red roses, love; pink roses, perfect happiness; and a single rose in full bloom, I love you.

photography credits

Polly Wreford pages 6–7, 8, 21, 22, 23 above left, 38, 39, 44, 46, 47, 51, 53 background, 54, 55, 56, 57, 58, 59

Christopher Drake pages 10, 12 left, 13, 18 main, 19, 24, 34, 41, 45

Debi Treloar pages 26, 33, 35, 36, 37

James Merrell pages 2, 20, 31, 42

David Montgomery pages 4–5, 28, 48, 49

Melanie Eclare pages 12 right, 14–15, 16

Pia Tryde pages 9, 11, 29

Caroline Arber pages 40 left, 50

Craig Fordham pages 60, 61

Caroline Hughes page 17 both

Tom Leighton pages 18 inset, 25

David Loftus pages 23 right, 32

Martin Brigdale page 30

David Brittain page 40 right

Dan Duchars page 43

Chris Everard page 27

Catherine Gratwicke page 23 below left

Ian Wallace page 53 left

location credits

Pages 10, 12 left, 45:
Chichi Meroni Fassio, Parnassus
t. +39 02 78 11 07

Pages 12 right, 14–15:
Mirabel Osler's garden in
Ludlow, Shropshire

Pages 13, 18 main, 24:
Enrica Stabile's garden
in Brunello, Italy
www.enricastabile.com

Page 16:
The garden of James Morris in
Bristol designed by Sue Berger
and Helen Phillips, Town Garden
Design, Bristol
t. +44 1179 423 843

Page 17:
Iden Croft Herbs
www.herbs-uk.com

Pages 33, 35–37:
Anna Massee of Het Grote
Avontuur's home in Amsterdam
Het Grote Avontuur
t. +31 20 6268597
www.hetgroteavontuur.nl

Pages 34, 41:
Ali Sharland's home in
Gloucestershire
Sharland & Lewis
t. +44 1666 500354
www.sharlandandlewis.com

index